SUSHI
MODOKI

SUSHI MODOKI

THE EXPERIMENT

NEW YORK

THE JAPANESE ART AND CRAFT OF
VEGAN SUSHI

iina

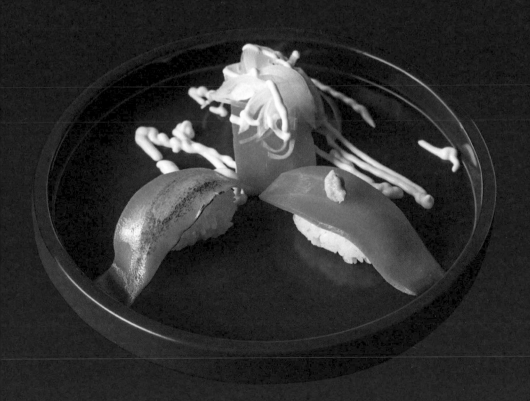

SUSHI MODOKI: *The Japanese Art and Craft of Vegan Sushi*
Copyright © 2017, 2019 by iina and Graphic-sha Publishing Co., Ltd.

First designed and published in Japan in 2017 by Graphic-sha Publishing Co., Ltd.
First published in North America in revised form by The Experiment, LLC, in 2019.
English-language rights arranged through Paper Crane Agency, Tokyo, Japan.

The Experiment, LLC
220 East 23rd Street, Suite 600, New York, NY 10010-4658 | theexperimentpublishing.com

This book contains the opinions and ideas of its author. It is intended to provide helpful and informative material on the subjects addressed in the book. It is sold with the understanding that the author and publisher are not engaged in rendering medical, health, or any other kind of personal professional services in the book. The author and publisher specifically disclaim all responsibility for any liability, loss, or risk—personal or otherwise—that is incurred as a consequence, directly or indirectly, of the use and application of any of the contents of this book.

THE EXPERIMENT and its colophon are registered trademarks of The Experiment, LLC. Many of the designations used by manufacturers and sellers to distinguish their products are claimed as trademarks. Where those designations appear in this book and The Experiment was aware of a trademark claim, the designations have been capitalized.

The Experiment's books are available at special discounts when purchased in bulk for premiums and sales promotions as well as for fund-raising or educational use. For details, contact us at info@theexperimentpublishing.com.

Library of Congress Cataloging-in-Publication Data

Names: iina, author.
Title: Sushi modoki : the Japanese art of crafting vegan sushi / iina.
Description: New York : The Experiment, 2019. | Includes index.
Identifiers: LCCN 2019025397 (print) | LCCN 2019025398 (ebook) | ISBN
    9781615196081 | ISBN 9781615196098 (ebook)
Subjects: LCSH: Vegan cooking--Japan. | Cooking, Japanese.
Classification: LCC TX724.5.J3 S29 2019 (print) | LCC TX724.5.J3 (ebook)
    | DDC 641.5/6362--dc23
LC record available at https://lccn.loc.gov/2019025397
LC ebook record available at https://lccn.loc.gov/2019025398

ISBN 978-1-61519-608-1
Ebook ISBN 978-1-61519-609-8

Original Japanese Edition Creative Staff
Author: iina
Original design and layout: Ryo Yoshinura & Kaho Magara (Yoshi-des)
Photography: Shinsaku Kato
Japanese edition editor: Yoko Koike (Graphic-sha Publishing)
English translation: Kevin Wilson
Special thanks: Mikano Katayama, Natsuki Tsukakoshi
English edition layout: Shinichi Ishioka
Foreign edition production & project management: Kumiko Sakamoto (Graphic-sha Publishing)

Cover design by Beth Bugler
Text design by Sarah Schneider
Cover and author photograph by Shinsaku Kato

Manufactured in China

First printing October 2019
10 9 8 7 6 5 4 3 2

CONTENTS

WELCOME TO SUSHI MODOKI

There's no Japanese food more iconic than sushi. There are many different varieties, including *nigirizushi* (thin slices of fish over rice), *chirashizushi* (rice bowls with sliced fish and chopped vegetables), *oshizushi* (sushi pressed into neat rectangles), and *inarizushi* (rice-stuffed deep-fried tofu), all of which are enjoyed daily in Japan.

The Japanese word *modoki* means "to mimic." Sushi modoki is sushi that mimics the color, taste, and texture of real sushi. But instead of fish, sushi modoki is made with vegetables.

All of the recipes in this book are for vegetable sushi, made with ingredients harvested from nature. With just a few simple tricks, you can turn vegetables into sushi that closely resembles the popular sushi dishes that normally require fish.

Everyone can enjoy sushi modoki, from vegetable-loving vegans, to genuine sushi lovers, to those who are allergic to or dislike the taste of seafood.

Making your own vegan sushi is easy and fun. I hope you and everyone you share this sushi with will be amazed by the recipes in this book.

iina

INGREDIENTS

Instead of fish, sushi modoki uses vegetables.
All seasonings are made from natural ingredients.

Vegetables

Please use fresh vegetables, just as traditional sushi would use fresh fish. Cook vegetables whole unless the recipe calls for something specific–for example, peeling or blanching. Most of the Japanese vegetables in these recipes, such as shiso leaves, can be found at your local Japanese grocery store. If you can't find *konnyaku*, a jelly made from the corm of the konjac root, you can use *shirataki* noodles to achieve a similar effect.

Seaweed

These recipes use sheets of nori (8½ × 7½ inches/21 × 19 cm) that are widely available at many grocery stores. Choose nori that has a rich flavor, preferably produced in Japan. If a sheet of nori becomes damp, you can lightly toast it by passing it over an open flame on the stove top before you assemble your sushi. Some recipes also call for kombu, a type of edible kelp with a savory flavor, and aonori, dried green laver seaweed often crushed into flakes.

The front of a nori sheet is smooth and the back is coarse. The coarse side should always face in when making sushi. For sushi rolls, place the nori sheet coarse side up on the sushi mat. Nori easily absorbs moisture, so serve your sushi immediately.

Tofu

Firm tofu is used in many recipes, but you'll also find fried tofu preparations, *aburaage* (fried tofu pockets) and *atsuage* (fried tofu cutlets). If you can't find these premade in Japanese grocery stores, you can use firm tofu to make your own.

Seasonings

Whenever possible, use seasonings that are additive-free and naturally fermented. Use unrefined sea salt. Instead of processed white sugar, I recommend using mirin (sweet rice wine), brown sugar, or maple syrup as a sweetener. Umeboshi, Japanese pickled plums, are also used in many recipes to add sweetness. Soy sauce can be used as a dipping sauce.

Oils

Please use unrefined oils. Many recipes in this book use flaxseed oil, which has a very distinctive flavor, in order to mimic the taste of seafood. Perilla oil is another good option.

UTENSILS

Use the utensils that you already have in your kitchen as best you can.
You will, however, need a sushi mat for making sushi rolls.

Wooden Rice Paddle
It is best to use a wooden rice paddle when mixing sushi vinegar and cooked rice. Soak your wooden rice paddle in water before use to prevent grains of rice from sticking to it.

Fan
Use a hand fan to cool down hot cooked rice. Large fans are best.

Sushi Mat
Ideal sushi mats are made of bamboo. After use, gently wash your sushi mat to remove grains stuck between the sticks. Dry your sushi mat completely before you put it away.

Molds
For oshi (pressed sushi), you can use a cake pan instead of a pressed sushi mold. Line your mold with plastic wrap so that the sushi comes out of the pan more easily.

MAKING SUSHI RICE

To make sushi, use rice that has just been cooked.

SUSHI RICE GUIDE

One piece of *nigirizushi* = about 1 heaping tablespoon (15 g)

One piece of *gunkanmaki* = about 1 heaping tablespoon (15 g)

One sushi roll = about ¾ cup (150 g), very lightly packed

¾ cup (150 g) uncooked rice should make enough for two sushi rolls

One hand roll = about 2 heaping tablespoons (30 g)

One piece of *inarizushi* = about 2 heaping tablespoons (30 g)

SUSHI RICE

Use short grain white Japanese rice for all recipes. This rice holds its flavor and quality even when it gets cold. It is often labeled as "sushi rice" in stores. Since sushi vinegar will be added to the cooked rice to make proper sushi rice, use slightly less water than the package directions suggest.

ADDING OTHER GRAINS

Some recipes call for sushi rice with black rice (Pink Roll, page 41; Ichimatsu Roll, page 51; Veggie Inari, page 79; and Eel Modoki Nigiri, page 22) or quinoa (Tazuna Roll, page 48, and Salad Chirashi, page 64). To add these grains, measure out 1½ cups (300 g) uncooked sushi rice and remove 2 tablespoons. Then add 2 tablespoons black rice or quinoa, as called for in the recipe. The soaking time and the amount of water is the same as that for regular short-grain rice.

BASIC SUSHI RICE

Makes 3 cups (600 g)

1½ cups (300 g) uncooked sushi-grade white rice

1¼-inch (3 cm) square piece dried kombu

3 tablespoons (45 ml) Sushi Vinegar (page 7)

Rice Cooker Method

1. Gently wash the rice in water to remove any rice bran or impurities. Rinse several times, until the water is no longer cloudy.

2. Transfer the washed rice to the inner pot of a rice cooker. Add 1½ cups (360 ml) water and the kombu; if your rice cooker has a water level indicator for cooking rice for sushi, add water to that line. Set aside for 30 minutes to 1 hour to soak.

3. Insert the inner pot into the rice cooker and turn it on.

4. When the rice is cooked, keep the cooker closed and leave for 10 to 15 minutes to steam.

5. Transfer the rice to a bowl. Fold the Sushi Vinegar into the rice using a wooden rice paddle. While folding, cool the rice using a fan to remove moisture. This will prevent it from becoming overly starchy.

6. Once the rice has become shiny and cooled to room temperature, cover the bowl with a dampened kitchen towel or paper towel to prevent the rice from drying out. Set aside until you are ready to make sushi, for no longer than a few hours.

Stove-Top Method

1. Put the rice in a bowl with water and wash gently. Rinse the rice several times, until the water is no longer cloudy, and transfer to a medium saucepan. Add 1½ cups water and the kombu. Let soak for 30 minutes.

2. Cover the pot and bring to a boil. Reduce the heat to low and simmer for about 5 minutes. Remove from the heat.

3. Let stand for 15 minutes while covered.

4. Remove the lid and gently fluff the rice with a spoon or spatula.

5. Transfer the rice to a bowl. Fold the Sushi Vinegar into the rice using a wooden rice paddle. While folding, cool the rice using a fan to remove moisture. This will prevent it from becoming overly starchy.

6. Once the rice has become shiny and cooled to room temperature, cover the bowl with a dampened kitchen towel or paper towel to prevent the rice from drying out. Set aside until you are ready to make sushi, for no longer than a few hours.

SUSHI VINEGAR

Makes about 1 cup plus 2 tablespoons (275 ml), enough for six batches Basic Sushi Rice

¾ cup (180 ml) apple cider vinegar

⅓ cup plus 1 tablespoon (95 ml) light maple syrup

2 tablespoons salt

Combine all of the ingredients in a small bowl. Mix well until the salt dissolves. You can also combine all the ingredients in a small jar with a lid and shake well until the salt dissolves.

NIGIRI

MAKING NIGIRI

Use plastic wrap if you find that forming sushi rice with your hands is difficult.

NIGIRIZUSHI

1. Prepare vinegar water (equal parts water and rice vinegar) in a small bowl. Dip your hands in.

2. Place the topping in the palm of your left hand. Use your right index finger to add a thin layer of wasabi to the topping.

3. Use your right hand to grab about 1 heaping tablespoon (15 g) of the sushi rice. Softly ball the rice in your palm and place it on the topping. Press down with your left thumb to make a dent in the center of the ball (see Tip).

4. Adjust the shape of the rice with your right thumb and index finger.

5. Flip the nigirizushi over so the topping is facing up. Adjust the shape using your right index and middle fingers.

EASIER METHOD
If you find forming rice with your hands difficult, you can use plastic wrap. Wrap the rice with plastic wrap and form the desired shape. Remove the plastic wrap and place the balled rice on a platter. Spread a thin layer of wasabi on the rice and then add the topping.

TIP: Making a dent in the balled rice allows it to easily fall apart in the mouth.

GUNKAN

1. Prepare vinegar water (equal parts water and rice vinegar) in a small bowl.

2. Cut a large nori sheet (about 8 × 7 inches/ 21 × 19 cm) into six equal strips.

3. Dip your hands in the vinegar water. Use your right hand to grab about 1 heaping tablespoon (15 g) of the sushi rice. Softly ball the rice in your palm.

4. Place the balled rice on a platter and wrap a nori strip around it. Add a few grains of rice where the nori overlaps. This will "glue" the end down.

5. Spoon on the desired topping.

MARINATED
TUNA
MODOKI
NIGIRI

FATTY TUNA
MODOKI
NIGIRI

TUNA
MODOKI
NIGIRI

TUNA MODOKI NIGIRI

Makes 8 pieces

TUNA MODOKI
1 red bell pepper, halved lengthwise, stemmed, seeded, and frozen for 8 hours or overnight

NIGIRI
⅔ cup (120 g) Basic Sushi Rice (page 6)

Wasabi

1. To make the Tuna Modoki, bring a small saucepan of water to boil over high heat. Add the frozen pepper halves skin-side-down and boil for 10 to 15 minutes, until the skin starts to wrinkle.

2. Transfer the pepper halves to a bowl of ice water to cool. Peel the skin off, beginning at the stem side. Cut each half lengthwise into four equal parts.

3. Assemble the nigirizushi (see page 10) with the rice, using each pepper piece as the topping. Spread some wasabi on top.

FATTY TUNA MODOKI NIGIRI

Makes 6 pieces

FATTY TUNA MODOKI
1 medium tomato (see Tip)

1 tablespoon flaxseed oil

NIGIRI
½ cup (90 g) Basic Sushi Rice (see page 6)

1. To make the Fatty Tuna Modoki, cut around the stem of the tomato and discard the stem and core. Cut a shallow X on the bottom of the tomato.

2. Bring a small saucepan of water to boil over high heat. Add the tomato. After a few seconds, transfer the tomato to a bowl of ice water to cool.

3. Peel off the skin, starting at the bottom where the X was cut.

4. Halve the tomato lengthwise. Cut each tomato half into three equal parts crosswise. Remove the seeds and transfer to a baking pan.

5. Pour the oil over the tomato and cover tightly with plastic wrap so that it touches the tomatoes. Let stand for about 15 minutes.

6. Assemble the nigirizushi (see page 10) with the rice, using each tomato slice as the topping.

TIP: Use tomatoes that are firm and not overly ripe.

MARINATED TUNA MODOKI NIGIRI

Makes 8 pieces

MARINATED TUNA
MODOKI

1 red bell pepper, halved
lengthwise, stemmed,
seeded, and frozen for
8 hours or overnight

2 tablespoons mirin

2 tablespoons sake

2 tablespoons soy sauce

NIGIRI

²/₃ cup (120 g) Basic
Sushi Rice (page 6)

Toasted white sesame
seeds

Red and White Pickled
Ginger (page 104),
optional

1. To make the Marinated Tuna Modoki, bring a small
saucepan of water to boil over high heat. Add the frozen
pepper halves skin-side-down and boil for 10 to
15 minutes, until the skin starts to wrinkle.

2. Transfer the pepper halves to a bowl of ice water to
cool. Peel the skin off, beginning at the stem side.

3. Bring the mirin, sake, and soy sauce to a simmer in a
small saucepan, then remove from the heat and allow
to cool.

4. Cut each pepper half lengthwise into four equal parts
and transfer to a baking pan. Pour the mirin marinade
over the pepper and cover tightly with plastic wrap so that
it touches the pepper. Marinate for 30 minutes to 1 hour.

5. Assemble the nigirizushi (see page 10) with the rice,
using each pepper piece as the topping. Sprinkle with
the sesame seeds. Add Red and White Pickled Ginger,
if desired.

SALMON MODOKI NIGIRI

Makes 10 pieces

SALMON MODOKI
½ medium carrot

1 tablespoon
flaxseed oil

NIGIRI
¾ cup (150 g) Basic
Sushi Rice (page 6)

Wasabi

Thinly sliced onion

Tofu Mayonnaise
(page 97)

1. To make the Salmon Modoki, use a mandoline to slice the carrot into 10 paper-thin slices (see Tips).

2. Use a vegetable steamer to steam the carrot slices for about a minute, until fork tender (see Tips). Spread them on a baking sheet.

3. Pour the oil over the carrot slices and cover tightly with plastic wrap so that it touches the carrots. Let stand for about 15 minutes.

4. Transfer a few slices to an oven-safe dish and sear with a kitchen torch.

5. Assemble the nigirizushi (see page 10) with the rice, using either seared or unseared carrot slices as the topping.

6. On the unseared Salmon Modoki, add the wasabi, onion slices, and Tofu Mayonnaise as desired.

TIPS: Using a mandoline to slice the carrots will create the perfect curve for nigirizushi.

Do not overcook the carrot slices–they will easily fall apart.

SALMON MODOKI NIGIRI

SCALLOP MODOKI NIGIRI

ABALONE MODOKI NIGIRI

SCALLOP MODOKI NIGIRI

SCALLOP MODOKI NIGIRI

Makes 4 pieces

SCALLOP MODOKI

2 large and thick-stemmed king oyster mushrooms

¾-inch (2 cm) piece dried kombu

Salt

NIGIRI

⅓ cup (60 g) Basic Sushi Rice (page 6)

Aonori (dried seaweed flakes)

1. To make the Scallop Modoki, cut each mushroom stem crosswise into two 1¼-inch (3 cm) slices (see Tip). Butterfly the slices (splitting each down the center but being careful not to cut through completely).

2. Fill a small saucepan with about ½ inch (1 cm) water. Add the mushroom slices, kombu, and salt. Cover and bring to a boil, then reduce the heat to low and simmer for 2 to 3 minutes.

3. Transfer two mushroom slices to an oven-safe dish. Sear with a kitchen torch.

4. Assemble the nigirizushi (see page 10) with the rice, using each butterflied mushroom slice as the topping.

5. Sprinkle the unseared Scallop Modoki with aonori.

TIP: If your mushroom stem slices are thick, they will end up just the right size, as they will shrink during the cooking process.

ABALONE MODOKI NIGIRI

Makes 4 pieces

ABALONE MODOKI

1 large and thick-stemmed king oyster mushroom

¾-inch (2 cm) piece dried kombu

Salt

NIGIRI

⅓ cup (60 g) Basic Sushi Rice (page 6)

4 lime slices

Red cabbage sprouts or other sprouts, optional

1. To make the Abalone Modoki, slice the stem of the mushroom diagonally into slices 1¼ inches (3 cm) thick. Score the slices on one side four or five times.

2. Fill a small saucepan with about ½ inch (1 cm) water. Add the mushroom slices, kombu, and salt. Cover and bring to a boil, then reduce the heat to low and simmer for 2 to 3 minutes.

3. Assemble the nigirizushi (see page 10) with the rice, using each mushroom slice as the topping. Garnish with the lime and sprouts, if desired.

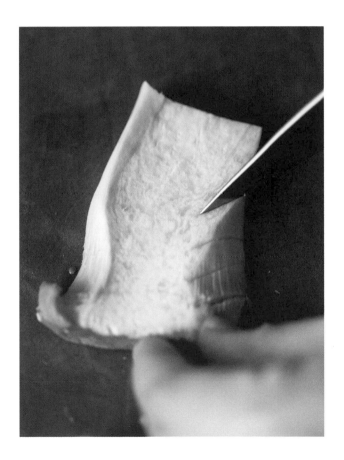

SQUID MODOKI NIGIRI

Makes 6 pieces

SQUID MODOKI

About half a 9-ounce (255 g) block white konnyaku (Japanese yam cake)

LEMON PEPPER SALT (OPTIONAL)

¼ teaspoon *moshio* (seaweed salt)

Ground black pepper

1 tablespoon lemon juice

NIGIRI

½ cup (90 g) Basic Sushi Rice (page 6)

1 green shiso leaf, cut in half

Grated ginger

Pitted umeboshi (pickled plum)

Japanese Chili Oil (page 97), optional (see Tip)

1. To make the Squid Modoki, slice the konnyaku diagonally into six slices thin enough that your finger is visible through it and score the surface of each slice several times along its length.

2. To make the Lemon Pepper Salt, if using, combine the seaweed salt and pepper in a small bowl. Stir in the lemon juice.

3. Assemble the nigirizushi (see page 10) with the rice, using each konnyaku slice as the topping. Top each of two pieces with a shiso leaf half. For the remaining four pieces, put a small amount of either grated ginger or umeboshi on top. If desired, serve with Lemon Pepper Salt or Japanese Chili Oil.

TIP: Konnyaku can be quite bland on its own, so enjoy it with flavorful dipping sauces.

EEL MODOKI NIGIRI

Makes 4 pieces

EEL MODOKI

2 tablespoons mirin

2 tablespoons Veggie
Dashi Soy Sauce
(page 98)

1 tablespoon sake

About 1 tablespoon
brown sugar (see Tips)

2 medium Japanese
eggplants, stemmed
and peeled (see Tips)

Ground black pepper

NIGIRI

Four nori strips, each
about 3 × 1 inch
(7 × 3 cm)

⅓ cup (60 g) Basic Sushi
Rice (page 6)

1. To make the Eel Modoki, combine the mirin, Veggie Dashi Soy Sauce, sake, sugar, and pepper in a small saucepan. Reduce the mixture by half over medium heat.

2. Steam the eggplants in a steamer for about 5 minutes, until a skewer smoothly pierces the eggplants. Transfer to a baking sheet and let cool.

3. Halve each eggplant lengthwise and score each half along its length with three cuts to flatten the eggplant.

4. Assemble the nigirizushi (see page 10) by placing a strip of nori between the rice and one of the flattened eggplant halves. Brush with the mirin marinade and sprinkle with pepper.

TIPS: Adjust the amount of sugar in the marinade to suit your preference.

You can also use one large Japanese eggplant, quartering it lengthwise and using each quarter as the topping.

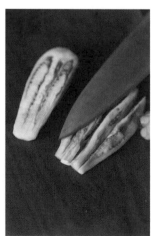

TAMAGO MODOKI NIGIRI:
JAPANESE OMELET

Makes 10 pieces

TAMAGO MODOKI
One 16-ounce (454 g) package firm tofu

½ cup (60 g) peeled, diced kabocha squash

1 tablespoon mirin

1 tablespoon potato starch

1 teaspoon cornstarch (see Tips)

1 teaspoon Veggie Dashi Soy Sauce (page 98)

⅛ teaspoon salt

NIGIRI
¾ cup (150 g) Basic Sushi Rice (page 6)

10 nori strips, each about 4 × ½ inch (10 × 1 cm)

Shibazuke (page 107), optional

1. **To make the Tamago Modoki,** freeze 11 ounces (300 g) of the tofu overnight (see Tips). Refrigerate the remaining 5 ounces (150 g) in a strainer over a bowl overnight to remove moisture.

2. Thaw the frozen tofu until soft. Remove any moisture by squeezing with both hands.

3. Steam the squash until tender.

4. Put all of the Tamago Modoki ingredients in a food processor and pulse until smooth.

5. Line a 9 × 5-inch (22 × 15 cm) baking pan with parchment paper and pour in the mixture. Smooth the surface.

6. Preheat the oven to 350°F (180°C). Bake for 20 to 25 minutes, until the top is golden brown.

7. Remove from the oven and let cool. Cut into 10 equal pieces.

8. **Assemble the nigirizushi** (see page 10) with the rice, using each "omelet" piece as the topping. Wrap with a nori strip as pictured. If desired, serve with Shibazuke.

TIPS: Freezing the tofu produces a perfect Japanese-style omelet texture.

If you don't have cornstarch on hand, you can increase the amount of potato starch instead.

If you wish to make your omelet modoki sweeter, just add brown sugar or raw cane sugar to the mixture.

SHIRAKO MODOKI GUNKAN:
COD MILT

Makes 8 pieces

SHIRAKO MODOKI

11 ounces (300 g)
firm tofu

¼ teaspoon salt

⅛ teaspoon aonori
(dried seaweed flakes)

GUNKAN

¼ cup (30 g)
grated daikon

⅛ teaspoon red
pepper flakes

⅔ cup (120 g) Basic
Sushi Rice (page 6)

8 nori strips, each about
7½ × 1½ inches
(19 × 3.5 cm)

Finely chopped scallion

Kombu Ponzu (page 98),
optional

1. To make the Shirako Modoki, place the tofu on a stack of paper towels in the refrigerator overnight to remove moisture.

2. Combine the tofu, salt, and aonori in a food processor and pulse until smooth.

3. To make the gunkanmaki, mix the daikon and red pepper flakes.

4. Assemble the gunkanmaki (see page 11) with the rice, using a pastry bag with a round tip to pipe the Shirako Modoki on top in a circular motion. Top with a small amount of the daikon mixture and scallion. Serve with Kombu Ponzu, if desired.

TIP: Be sure to thoroughly remove any moisture from the tofu before making the tofu paste.

NEGITORO MODOKI GUNKAN: *FATTY TUNA WITH CHOPPED SCALLION*

Makes 6 pieces

NEGITORO MODOKI

1 plum tomato

¼ cup (30 g) minced avocado, almost roughly mashed

¼ cup (20 g) finely chopped scallions

1 tablespoon flaxseed oil

GUNKAN

½ cup (90 g) Basic Sushi Rice (page 6)

6 nori strips, each about 7½ × 1½ inches (19 × 3.5 cm)

Finely chopped scallions

1. To make the Negitoro Modoki, cut around the tomato stem and discard the stem and core. Cut a shallow X on the bottom of the tomato.

2. Add enough water to cover the tomato in a saucepan and bring to a boil. Drop the tomato in the boiling water for a few seconds, then transfer to a bowl of ice water to cool.

3. Peel off the tomato skin, starting at the bottom where the X was cut.

4. Finely chop the tomato and mix with the avocado in a small bowl.

5. Add the scallions and oil and stir to combine.

6. Assemble the gunkanmaki (see page 11) with the rice, using the Negitoro Modoki as the topping. Top with additional scallions.

TOROTAKU MODOKI GUNKAN: FATTY TUNA WITH PICKLED DAIKON

Makes 8 pieces

TOROTAKU MODOKI

1 small tomato (about 3½ ounces/100 g)

¼ cup (30 g) minced avocado, almost roughly mashed

¼ cup (20 g) finely chopped scallions

1 tablespoon flaxseed oil

GUNKAN

⅔ cup (120 g) Basic Sushi Rice (page 6)

8 nori strips, each about 7½ × 1½ inches (19 × 3.5 cm)

⅔ cup (80 g) Takuan (pickled daikon, page 105), julienned

1. To make the Torotaku Modoki, cut around the tomato stem and discard the stem core. Cut a shallow X on the bottom of the tomato.

2. Add enough water to cover the tomato in a saucepan and bring to a boil. Drop the tomato in the boiling water for a few seconds, then transfer to a bowl of ice water to cool.

3. Peel off the tomato skin, starting at the bottom where the X was cut.

4. Finely chop the tomato and mix with the avocado in a small bowl.

5. Add the scallion and oil and stir to combine.

6. Assemble the gunkanmaki (see page 11) with the rice. Add some of the Takuan and top with the Torotaku Modoki.

NEGITORO MODOKI NIGIRI

TOROTAKU MODOKI NIGIRI

UNI MODOKI GUNKAN: *SEA URCHIN*

Makes 8 pieces

UNI MODOKI

1 cup (130 g) diced carrot

¾ cup (90 g) peeled, diced kabocha squash

2 tablespoons canola oil

2 teaspoons miso

2 teaspoons (10 g) sake *kasu* (see Tips)

1½ teaspoons (3 g) dried hijiki, soaked in water for 30 minutes

½ teaspoon salt

GUNKAN

⅔ cup (120 g) Basic Sushi Rice (page 6)

8 nori strips, each about 7½ × 1½ inches (19 × 3.5 cm)

8 cucumber slices

1. To make the Uni Modoki, steam the carrot and squash until soft, about 5 minutes.

2. Add all of the Uni Modoki ingredients to a food processor and pulse until smooth.

3. Assemble the gunkanmaki (see page 11) with the rice, adding a cucumber slice and topping with the Uni Modoki.

TIPS: Sake kasu is the lees left over from unrefined sake production. This recipe uses sake kasu to produce a grainy sea urchin-like flavor.

Enjoy leftovers with crackers or veggie sticks.

TOBIKO MODOKI GUNKAN:
FLYING FISH ROE

Makes 6 pieces

TOBIKO MODOKI

¼ cup (50 g) amaranth

¾ cup plus 1 tablespoon
(200 ml) carrot juice

Pinch of salt

GUNKAN

½ cup (90 g) Basic Sushi
Rice (page 6)

6 nori strips, each about
7½ × 1½ inches (19 × 3.5 cm)

6 cucumber slices

1. To make the Tobiko Modoki, combine all the Tobiko Modoki ingredients in a small saucepan. Heat on low and simmer for 10 to 15 minutes, uncovered, until the liquid has almost completely evaporated and the amaranth grains no longer stick together. If there is still liquid in the pan after 10 minutes, turn up the heat so the liquid evaporates, stirring constantly. Remove from the heat, cover, and let stand for about 10 minutes. Then uncover and allow to cool.

2. Assemble the gunkanmaki (see page 11) with the rice, adding a cucumber slice and topping with the Tobiko Modoki.

IKA MODOKI NATTO GUNKAN: *SQUID WITH NATTO*

Makes 6 pieces

IKA MODOKI

2 ounces (60 g) white konnyaku

YUZU PEPPER SOY SAUCE

2 teaspoons Veggie Dashi (page 91)

1 teaspoon light soy sauce

1/8 teaspoon yuzu *kosho* (yuzu pepper seasoning)

GUNKAN

1/2 cup (90 g) Basic Sushi Rice (page 6)

6 nori strips, each about 7½ × 1½ inches (19 × 3.5 cm)

1 cup plus 1 tablespoon (200 g) natto (fermented, crushed soybeans)

Umami Malted Rice (page 98), optional

1. To make the Ika Modoki, cut the konnyaku into sticks ¼ inch (5 mm) wide. Set aside on a paper towel to remove moisture.

2. To make the Yuzu Pepper Soy Sauce, if using, combine the Veggie Dashi and soy sauce in a small bowl. Add the yuzu kosho and stir to combine.

3. Assemble the gunkanmaki (see page 11) with the rice, topping with the natto and konnyaku sticks. Serve with Umami Malted Rice and Yuzu Pepper Soy Sauce, if desired.

VARIATION
IKA MODOKI OKRA NIGIRI

You can make these with 3 thinly sliced okra pods instead of the natto.

TUNA CORN MODOKI GUNKAN

Makes 6 pieces

TUNA CORN MODOKI

1 ounce (30 g) seitan

2 tablespoons (20 g) minced onion

½ zucchini

⅓ cup (60 g) cooked chickpeas

½ cup (120 g) Tofu Mayonnaise (page 97)

⅓ cup (50 g) corn kernels

¼ teaspoon salt

Ground black pepper

GUNKAN

½ cup (90 g) Basic Sushi Rice (page 6)

Cayenne pepper

1. To make the Tuna Corn Modoki, soak the seitan in a bowl of water for 10 to 15 minutes. Lightly squeeze to remove excess moisture and then tear into small pieces.

2. Place the onion in a bowl of water. Drain and wrap in paper towel to remove moisture.

3. Use a mandoline to cut the zucchini into long slices. Salt the zucchini slices generously (see Tip, page 35).

4. Pulse the chickpeas and seitan in a food processor until smooth.

5. Combine the chickpea mixture, onion, Tofu Mayonnaise, corn, salt, and pepper to taste in a bowl.

6. Assemble the gunkanmaki (see page 11) with the rice, topping with the Tuna Corn Modoki and a sprinkle of cayenne pepper.

SUSHI MODOKI

SEAFOOD SALAD MODOKI GUNKAN

Makes 6 pieces

SEAFOOD SALAD
MODOKI

⅓ cup (40 g) diced
cucumber (¼-inch/
5 mm cubes)

2 tablespoons (20 g)
diced red bell pepper
(¼-inch/5 mm cubes)

2 tablespoons (20 g)
diced red onion
(¼-inch/5 mm cubes)

¼ teaspoon salt, plus
more for the zucchini

3 slices (60 g) Squid
Modoki (page 21)

1 or 2 slices (40 g)
Scallop Modoki
(page 18)

½ zucchini

¼ cup (60 g) Tofu
Mayonnaise (page 97)

GUNKAN

½ cup (90 g) Basic Sushi
Rice (page 6)

2 tablespoons (30 g)
Tobiko Modoki
(page 31)

Cayenne pepper

1. To make the Seafood Salad Modoki, combine the cucumber, bell pepper, and onion in a small bowl. Sprinkle with the salt. Wrap in a paper towel and squeeze to remove excess moisture.

2. Dice the Squid and Scallop Modoki toppings into ¼-inch (5 mm) cubes.

3. Use a mandoline to cut the zucchini into long slices, then sprinkle with salt (see Tips).

4. Combine the diced vegetables, including the Squid and Scallop Modoki, with the Tofu Mayonnaise in a small bowl.

5. Assemble the gunkanmaki (see page 11) with the rice, topping with the Seafood Salad Modoki, Tobiko Modoki, and a sprinkle of cayenne pepper.

TIPS: Sprinkling some salt on the zucchini slices allows them to be used like strips of nori.

Use the vegetable peels, cores, stems, and ends left over from making the Seafood Salad Modoki to make Roasted Vegetable Broth (page 92).

SUSHI ROLLS

MAKING SUSHI ROLLS

The rule of thumb for making sushi rolls is to be careful not to use too much rice or filling. When using multiple fillings, assemble them in layers. This will show the beautiful layers when the roll is cut into pieces.

FUTOMAKI (THICK SUSHI ROLLS)

1. Prepare vinegar water (equal parts water and rice vinegar) in a small bowl.

2. Place a sushi mat flat-side-up on a flat working surface. Place a sheet of nori coarse-side-up on top, aligning the nori and the mat.

3. Moisten your hands well with vinegar water. Spread ¾ cup (150 g) sushi rice on the nori, leaving a ⅜-inch (1 cm) margin on the near side and a ⅝-inch (1.5 cm) margin on the far side.

4. Arrange the fillings across the sushi rice slightly below the middle. Add multiple fillings in layers.

5. Pick up the near side of the mat and roll it over the filling and away from you. With your left hand, pull up on the far side of the mat while holding the rolled portion of the mat to tighten the roll and continue rolling.

6. Set the roll aside for a couple of minutes before cutting to the desired size (this will make it easier to slice).

TIP: Prepare a damp kitchen towel and wipe off the blade of your knife as you slice. This will prevent grains of rice from sticking to the blade.

SUSHI MODOKI

TEMAKIZUSHI (HAND ROLLS)

1. Prepare vinegar water (equal parts water and rice vinegar) in a small bowl.

2. Cut a large nori sheet (about 8 × 7 inches/21 × 19 cm) in half crosswise. Moisten your hands well with vinegar water.

3. Holding one of the half sheets with the coarse side up and the upper left corner pointing up, spread 2 heaping tablespoons (30 g) sushi rice over it. Arrange the fillings diagonally.

4. Bring the bottom left corner of the nori up over the rice and fillings, creating a triangle. Then overlap the top left and top right corners of the nori.

RAINBOW ROLL

Makes 1 roll

¼ medium carrot

½ cup (30 g) shredded red cabbage

Salt

¼ cucumber

¼ avocado

⅛ red bell pepper

⅛ yellow bell pepper

1 ounce (30 g) mizuna or other mustard greens

One 8 × 7-inch (21 × 19 cm) nori sheet

¾ cup (150 g) Basic Sushi Rice (page 6)

Cilantro Sauce (page 100), optional

1. Julienne the carrot and mix with the cabbage. Sprinkle with some salt.

2. Quarter the cucumber lengthwise. Dice the avocado and peppers into ¼-inch (5 mm) cubes. Trim the mizuna to the same width as the nori sheet.

3. Assemble the futomaki (see page 38), using the vegetables as the filling (see Tip). Serve with Cilantro Sauce, if desired.

TIP: Since the filling is made up of seven different items, you can adjust the amounts of each item to make it easier to roll.

SUSHI MODOKI

PINK ROLL

Makes 1 roll

RED CABBAGE
SLAW
Scant 1½ cups (100 g)
shredded red cabbage

½ garlic clove, grated

2 teaspoons lemon juice

2 teaspoons olive oil

½ teaspoon salt

Pinch of white pepper

MAKI
One 8 × 7-inch
(21 × 19 cm) nori sheet

¾ cup (150 g) Basic
Sushi Rice (page 6)
with added black rice
(see page 5)

⅓ cup (50 g) Shibazuke
(page 107)

1 ounce (30 g) radishes
or watermelon radishes
(about 6 medium),
julienned

1. To make the Red Cabbage Slaw, combine all the ingredients in a storage bag and seal it. Lightly knead the bag from the outside. Unseal and remove air from the storage bag, then seal it again. Refrigerate overnight. (This will make enough for two rolls and will keep for a week in the refrigerator.)

2. To assemble the futomaki, evenly spread the rice mixture on the nori. Since this is an inside-out roll, spread the rice over the nori without leaving any gaps at the edges.

3. Cover the rice with plastic wrap and flip it over onto the sushi mat so the nori is facing up.

4. Arrange the Red Cabbage Slaw, Shibazuke, and radishes in layers on the nori. Roll the mat but be careful not to roll the plastic wrap up inside. Set the roll aside for a couple of minutes, then cut to the desired size.

TIP: Black rice and red cabbage contain a purple phytochemical called anthocyanin. Adding acid (such as lemon juice) will turn them a vibrant pink.

KIMBAP MODOKI ROLL

Makes 1 roll

BBQ MODOKI

1 ounce (30 g) seitan

3 garlic cloves, grated

2-inch (5 cm) piece of ginger, grated

1½ teaspoons Veggie Dashi Soy Sauce (page 98)

1 teaspoon sesame oil

½ teaspoon roasted white sesame seeds

KOREAN-STYLE CARROTS

1 scant cup (100 g) julienned carrot

1 teaspoon sesame oil

¼ teaspoon salt

KOREAN-STYLE MUSTARD GREENS

Salt

3½ ounces (100 g) Japanese mustard spinach (*komatsuna*) or mustard greens

1 teaspoon sesame oil

KOREAN-STYLE NORI

Sesame oil

One 8 × 7-inch (21 × 19 cm) nori sheet

Roasted salt or kosher salt (see Tips)

MAKI

¾ cup (150 g) Basic Sushi Rice (page 6)

Two 8 × ½-inch (20 × 1 cm) strips Tamago Modoki (page 24), about 1 ounce (30 g)

Roasted white and black sesame seeds

1. To make the BBQ Modoki, combine all ingredients except the oil and sesame seeds in a small saucepan with a scant ½ cup (100 ml) water. Heat on low and simmer until the seitan soaks up all the liquid, then remove from heat. Add the oil and sesame seeds and mix.

2. To make the Korean-Style Carrots, mix the carrot, oil, and salt in a small bowl. Let stand until the carrots wilt a little. (This makes enough for three rolls.)

3. To make the Korean-Style Mustard Greens, bring a pot of salted water to a boil, add the greens to the pot, and boil for about 15 seconds. Then plunge into a bowl of cold water. Let cool, then pat dry. Cut to match the width of the nori sheet. Season with the oil and salt to taste. (This makes enough for three rolls.)

4. To make the Korean-Style Nori, use a pastry brush or the back of a spoon to brush sesame oil onto both sides of the nori sheet. Place in a medium sauté pan and lightly toast over low heat. Sprinkle salt on both sides.

5. Assemble the futomaki (see page 38) with the rice, layering the Tamago Modoki, BBQ Modoki, Korean-Style Carrots, and Korean-Style Mustard Greens as the filling. Sprinkle with roasted sesame seeds.

TIPS: For the seasoned nori, roasted salt is best because it has less moisture than other types of salt.

You can also use kimchi and Takuan (page 105) for the fillings.

VEGGIE TEMPURA ROLL

Makes 1 roll

TEMPURA BATTER
⅓ cup plus 1 tablespoon
(50 g) all-purpose flour

⅓ cup (80 ml) ice water

½ teaspoon vinegar

¼ teaspoon salt

VEGGIE TEMPURA
3 ounces (80 g) green beans

⅓ cup (50 g) corn kernels

1 teaspoon all-purpose flour

Canola oil

MAKI
One 8 × 7-inch (21 × 19 cm)
nori sheet

¾ cup (150 g) Basic Sushi Rice
(page 6)

Daikon Sauce (page 100),
optional

1. To make the Tempura Batter, combine all the
ingredients in a medium bowl and mix well.

2. To make the Veggie Tempura, combine the
green beans and corn with the flour. Pour the batter
over them.

3. Heat as much canola oil as you'd like for frying the
vegetables in a frying pan over high heat to 350°F
(180°C). Add the battered vegetables and fry until
golden brown.

4. Assemble the futomaki (see page 38) with the
rice, using the Veggie Tempura as the filling. Serve
with Daikon Sauce, if desired.

SHRIMP TEMPURA MODOKI ROLL

Makes 2 rolls

SHRIMP TEMPURA
MODOKI
One 9-ounce (255 g)
block white konnyaku

1 medium carrot

½ teaspoon salt

Pinch of aonori (dried
seaweed flakes)

1 recipe Tempura Batter
(page 44)

Canola oil

MAKI
Two 8 × 7-inch (21 × 19 cm)
nori sheets

1½ cups (300 g) Basic
Sushi Rice (page 6)

4 lettuce leaves

Daikon Sauce (page 100),
optional

1. To make the Shrimp Tempura Modoki, tear the konnyaku block into five equal parts lengthwise with your hands. Cut the carrot into five pieces for the "shrimp" tails.

2. Combine the konnyaku and carrot in a small saucepan with a scant ½ cup (100 ml) water, the salt, and aonori. Bring to a boil and cook until the water has evaporated. Set aside to cool.

3. Assemble the "shrimp" by pushing a carrot piece into a konnyaku piece.

4. Make the Tempura Batter. Heat as much canola oil as you'd like for frying the "shrimp" in a pan over high heat to 350°F (180°C). Coat each "shrimp" with batter and fry until golden brown.

5. Assemble two futomaki (see page 38) with the rice, using the lettuce and Shrimp Tempura Modoki as the filling. Serve with Daikon Sauce, if desired.

CAULIFLOWER ROLL

Makes 1 roll

5 ounces (150 g) cauliflower florets

⅓ cucumber

¼ cup (50 g) Tofu Cream Cheese (page 100)

¾ ounce (20 g) daikon radish sprouts or other sprouts

1 teaspoon Sushi Vinegar (page 7)

Two 8 × 7-inch (21 × 19 cm) nori sheets (see Tip)

4 or 5 pieces Salmon Modoki topping (page 15)

1. Chop the cauliflower into bite-size pieces. Steam in a steamer for about a minute over high heat. Set aside to cool.

2. Cut the cucumber lengthwise into six equal parts. Cut the Tofu Cream Cheese into sticks ½ inch (1 cm) wide.

3. Transfer the cauliflower to a food processor. Pulse until the florets are the size of a grain of rice. Add the Sushi Vinegar and mix.

4. Assemble the futomaki (see page 38) but stack both nori sheets on the sushi mat and spread the cauliflower (instead of sushi rice) over the nori, using the cucumber, sprouts, Salmon Modoki topping, and Tofu Cream Cheese as the filling.

TIP: Moisture in the cauliflower will weaken the nori and cause breakage, so double the nori for this roll to reinforce it.

ALFALFA SPROUT ROLL

Makes 1 roll

⅓ avocado (50 g)

¼ red bell pepper (30 g)

2 scallions

One 8 × 7-inch (21 × 19 cm) nori sheet

1 ounce (30 g) alfalfa sprouts (about 1 cup)

Spicy Mayonnaise (page 97), optional

1. Cut the avocado and pepper into sticks ¼-inch (5 mm) wide. Cut the scallions to the same width as the nori sheet.

2. Assemble the futomaki (see page 38) but spread the alfalfa sprouts (instead of sushi rice) on the nori, using the avocado, pepper, and scallions as the filling. Apply water along the end of the nori to glue it together. Serve with Spicy Mayonnaise, if desired.

TIP: To prevent the alfalfa sprouts from wilting, use unseasoned vegetables for this roll.

TAZUNA ROLL: *STRIPED ROLL*

Makes 1 roll

½ cucumber

⅙ avocado

4 slices Tuna Modoki
(page 13)

4 slices Salmon Modoki
(page 15)

2 cups (400 g) Basic
Sushi Rice (page 6)
with added quinoa
(see page 5)

Tofu Mayonnaise
(page 97)

Finely chopped parsley

1. Thinly slice the cucumber and avocado lengthwise.

2. Place plastic wrap on a sushi mat. Arrange the cucumber, avocado, Tuna Modoki, and Salmon Modoki, alternating, on a diagonal across the plastic wrap.

3. Spread the rice and quinoa on top (see Tip) and roll, being careful not to roll the plastic wrap up inside.

4. Transfer to a platter and remove the plastic wrap. Drizzle Tofu Mayonnaise over the roll and sprinkle with the parsley.

TIP: Arrange the sushi rice with quinoa in a cylinder shape to make rolling easier.

TAZUNA ROLL

ICHIMATSU ROLL: *CHECKERED ROLL*

Makes 2 rolls

Generous ¾ cup (160 g)
Basic Sushi Rice
(page 6; see Tips)

3½ ounces (100 g)
firm tofu

Scant 1 cup (230 ml)
canola oil

¾ cup (100 g) Takuan
(page 105)

Two 8 × 7-inch
(21 × 19 cm) nori sheets

Red and White Pickled
Ginger (page 104),
optional

1. Using a paper towel, press out all excess moisture from the tofu, then cut into large cubes.

2. Heat the oil in a sauté pan over medium-high heat and add the tofu. Deep-fry until golden brown, turning once or twice. Drain on paper towels and let cool.

3. Cut the tofu and Takuan into sticks ½-inch (1 cm) wide.

4. Place the nori on the sushi mat, coarse side up. Place the tofu along the bottom edge of the nori, without leaving a margin. Next to the tofu, add 3 tablespoons of the rice in a cylinder shape. On top of the tofu, add 3 tablespoons of the rice. On top of the first layer of rice, add more tofu. Using your hands, adjust the shape of the filling into a square.

5. Roll around the square; as you create corners and sides, adjust the shape over the mat.

6. Set the roll aside for a couple of minutes, then cut to the desired size.

7. Make another roll, this time with Takuan instead of tofu.

8. Serve with Red and White Pickled Ginger, if desired.

TIPS: Use half Basic Sushi Rice (page 6) and half Basic Sushi Rice with added black rice (see page 5) for a colorful variation.

Tamago Modoki (page 24) also tastes great in this roll.

HAND ROLL PARTY

Fill your table with platters of vegetables, fruits, rice, and dipping sauces. Invite your friends over for a hand roll party!

Serves 3

SAUTÉED ASPARAGUS WITH LEMON

1 tablespoon olive oil

5 asparagus stalks, trimmed and halved crosswise

1½ teaspoons lemon juice

⅛ teaspoon ground cumin

Salt and ground black pepper

CURRY BURDOCK ROOT

1 tablespoon sesame oil

5½ ounces (150 g) burdock root, julienned

1 large carrot (about 70 g), julienned

1 tablespoon mirin (sweet rice wine)

1 tablespoon soy sauce

2 teaspoons curry powder

TEMAKI

Nori sheets, rice paper wrappers (see Tip), and lettuce leaves for wrapping

3 cups (600 g) Basic Sushi Rice (page 6)

Vegetables, such as cucumbers, carrots, and peppers

Fruit, such as strawberries, kiwi, and mango

Tofu Cream Cheese (page 100)

Dipping sauces, such as Korean-Style Sweet and Spicy Miso (page 101), Sriracha (page 101), Maple-Balsamic Sauce (page 103), and Tapenade (page 103)

1. To make the Sautéed Asparagus with Lemon, heat the olive oil in a skillet over medium heat. Sauté the asparagus until browned. Reduce the heat to low. Add the lemon juice and cumin. Toss until coated. Add salt and pepper to taste. Remove from the heat and set aside.

2. To make the Curry Burdock Root, heat the sesame oil in a skillet over medium heat. Sauté the carrot and burdock until they begin to soften. Add the mirin, soy sauce, and curry powder. Increase the heat to medium-high and reduce, simmering until most of the liquid evaporates. Remove from the heat and set aside.

3. To assemble the temakizushi (see page 39), have guests layer fillings of their choice (including the asparagus and burdock) on the nori, lettuce, or rice paper and rice. Drizzle some sauce over the fillings, wrap, and enjoy immediately, or dip in sauce while eating.

TIP: Rice paper makes beautiful hand rolls because the fillings are visible underneath. Once rehydrated, the rice paper will become pliable and sticky. Place wet paper towels on a working surface to make it easier to make your hand rolls.

CHIRASHI

SEAFOOD MODOKI
CHIRASHI

GREEN VEGETABLE CHIRASHI

Serves 4

4 ounces (120 g) watercress (about 2 bunches)

3 tablespoons (45 ml) Sushi Vinegar (page 7)

¾ cup canned or 3½ ounces cooked fresh (100 g) bamboo shoots, sliced ⅛ inch (4 mm) wide

1½ teaspoons soy sauce

1 generous cup (80 g) broccoli florets

5 sugar snap peas, split lengthwise

3 brussels sprouts, halved

1½ cups (300 g) Basic Sushi Rice (page 6), kept warm

¼ teaspoon salt

1. Blanch the watercress, then drain. Combine with the Sushi Vinegar and salt in a food processor and pulse until smooth.

2. Combine the bamboo shoots, soy sauce, and 3 tablespoons water. Simmer on low until the liquid is reduced. Remove from the heat and set aside.

3. Blanch the broccoli, sugar snap peas, and brussels sprouts in boiling salted water. Drain when the vegetables are cooked but still crisp.

4. Put the hot rice in a bowl. Add the Sushi Vinegar and bamboo shoots and use a rice paddle to fold into the rice.

5. Transfer to a serving platter. Top with the broccoli, sugar snap peas, and brussels sprouts.

SEAFOOD MODOKI CHIRASHI

Serves 4

2 slices Tuna Modoki
(page 13)

2 slices Salmon Modoki
(page 15)

2 slices Scallop Modoki
(page 18)

2 slices Abalone Modoki
(page 19)

2 slices Squid Modoki
(page 21)

Tobiko Modoki (page 31)

6 shiso leaves

Daikon

1½ cups (300 g) Basic
Sushi Rice (page 6)

½ teaspoon toasted
white sesame seeds

Wasabi

Red and White Pickled
Ginger (page 104)

1. Dice each modoki slice into bite-size pieces. Julienne five of the shiso leaves. Use a mandoline to julienne as much of the daikon as desired.

2. Place the sushi rice on a serving platter. Arrange the modoki pieces, shiso leaves, and daikon on top. Sprinkle with the sesame seeds. Place the remaining shiso leaf on the edge of the platter and add wasabi and Red and White Pickled Ginger on top.

TIPS: Sprinkle shredded nori on the rice before topping to enhance the flavor.

Drizzle some soy sauce mixed with wasabi on top before eating.

SALAD CHIRASHI

Serves 4

Scant ½ cup (60 g) chopped red and yellow bell peppers (½-inch/ 1 cm cubes)

¾ cup (80 g) chopped cucumber (½-inch/1 cm cubes)

3 tablespoons (45 ml) Sushi Vinegar (page 7)

VEGAN CAESAR DRESSING

Scant ¼ cup (50 g) Tofu Mayonnaise (page 97)

1 tablespoon lemon juice

½ teaspoon light maple syrup

¼ teaspoon garlic powder

½ teaspoon salt

Ground black pepper

CHIRASHI

1 ounce (30 g) radishes (about 6 medium) or watermelon radishes

1½ cups (300 g) Basic Sushi Rice with added quinoa (see page 5), kept warm

Leafy greens, such as watercress or lettuce

Red cabbage sprouts (about ⅓ ounce/10 g)

1. Combine the bell peppers, cucumbers, and Sushi Vinegar in a medium bowl and marinate for a few hours.

2. To make the Vegan Caesar Dressing, combine all the ingredients in a small bowl and mix well. Transfer to a clean jar with a lid. (This will keep for a week in the refrigerator.)

3. To assemble the chirashizushi, use a mandoline to thinly slice the radishes. Then julienne.

4. Add the hot rice and quinoa to the bowl with the vinegar and vegetables and use a rice paddle to fold the vegetables in.

5. Transfer to a serving platter. Arrange the greens and sprouts on top. Add the radish and dress with the Vegan Caesar Dressing.

TIPS: Arrange herbs and leafy greens of your choice over the rice like a salad.

Black olives and seaweed are other delicious toppings.

GOMOKU MODOKI CHIRASHI

Serves 4

STEWED VEGETABLES

1 lotus root (about 3½ ounces/
100 g)

½ piece aburaage (fried tofu
pocket; see page 70), halved
lengthwise and cut across into
thin strips

1 small carrot (about 2 ounces/
50 g), julienned

1 ounce (30 g) shiitake mushrooms
(about 2 small), thinly sliced

Scant ½ cup (100 ml) Veggie Dashi
(page 91)

2 tablespoons mirin

2 tablespoons soy sauce

KINSHI TAMAGO MODOKI:
SHREDDED EGG CRÊPES

⅓ cup (50 g) peeled, diced kabocha
squash, steamed

2½ tablespoons rice flour

1 tablespoon potato starch

Pinch of salt

SAKURA DENBU MODOKI:
FLAKED CODFISH

2 ounces (50 g) strawberries (about
4 medium), hulled

2 tablespoons mirin

1 tablespoon brown sugar or
granulated sugar

1 tablespoon sake

⅛ teaspoon salt

3½ ounces (100 g) fresh okara
(soy pulp)

PLUM VINEGAR LOTUS ROOT

½ lotus root (about 2 ounces/50 g)

2 tablespoons ume plum vinegar or
red wine vinegar

1 tablespoon mirin

CHIRASHI

3 cups (600 g) Basic Sushi Rice
(page 6)

5 snow pea pods, boiled and
julienned diagonally

1. To make the Stewed Vegetables, halve the
lotus root lengthwise, then cut crosswise
into thin slices. Combine all the ingredients
in a saucepan. Simmer on low until all the
liquid has been reduced. Remove from the
heat and set aside.

2. To make the Kinshi Tamago Modoki,
preheat the oven to 350°F (180°C).

3. Combine all the ingredients along with
¼ cup (60 ml) water in a food processor and
pulse until smooth. Pour into a 9 × 5-inch
(21 × 15 cm) baking pan and spread evenly.
Bake for 7 to 8 minutes.

4. Remove from the oven and allow to cool.
Cut into thin slices.

5. To make the Sakura Denbu Modoki, combine all the ingredients except the okara in a food processor and pulse to mix.

6. Add all the ingredients to a skillet over low heat and cook until the okara becomes dry and flaky. Remove from the heat and set aside.

7. To make the Plum Vinegar Lotus Root, slice the lotus root into slices ⅛ inch (4 mm) thin. Make notches along the circumference of each slice to create a flower shape.

8. Combine all the ingredients in a small saucepan and heat over medium. Simmer, while stirring, until the lotus root is cooked through but still has a crunchy texture. Remove from the heat and set aside. These will keep for up to 10 days in the refrigerator.

9. To make the Chirashizushi, put the rice in a bowl. Fold the Stewed Vegetables into the rice and stir.

10. Top with the Kinshi Tamago Modoki, Sakura Denbu Modoki, three or four slices of the Plum Vinegar Lotus Root, and the pea pods.

INARI

MAKING INARI

PREPARING ABURAAGE (DEEP-FRIED TOFU POCKETS)

Prepare aburaage the day before you plan to make inari.

1. Bring water to a boil in a saucepan. Add the aburaage and boil for about 5 minutes to reduce oiliness. Drain in a colander and let cool. Remove moisture by pressing the aburaage with your hands.

2. Slice the aburaage in half. Combine the stew seasoning (as indicated in each recipe) and the aburaage in a saucepan. Simmer on low until almost all liquid has evaporated. Remove from the heat and let cool.

3. Lightly squeeze the aburaage to remove excess liquid and place on a cutting board. Roll a chopstick over the aburaage to make opening them easier.

4. Carefully open the aburaage from the cut edge, leaving the other three sides intact.

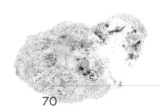

STUFFING THE ABURAAGE

Lightly ball sushi rice and stuff it inside the aburaage. If you find it easier, you can use the aburaage inside out.

1. Prepare vinegar water (equal parts water and rice vinegar) in a small bowl. Moisten your hands in the vinegar water.

2. Shape 2 heaping tablespoons (30 g) sushi rice into an oblong ball. Stuff it inside the aburaage and fold in the edge.

TIP: Push the center of the inarizushi down with your thumb, making a dent to create a soft texture.

SHISO HIJIKI INARI

Makes 8 pieces

4 pieces aburaage, prepared the day before

¾ cup plus 1 tablespoon (200 ml) apple juice (see Tips)

2 tablespoons mirin

2 tablespoons Veggie Dashi Soy Sauce (page 98)

1¼ cups (240 g) Basic Sushi Rice (page 6)

1 batch Shiso Hijiki (page 104)

Red and White Pickled Ginger (page 104), optional

1. Bring water to a boil in a saucepan. Add the aburaage and boil for about 5 minutes to reduce oiliness. Drain, cool, press to remove moisture, and cut in half.

2. Combine the apple juice, mirin, Veggie Dashi Soy Sauce, and aburaage in a saucepan. Simmer on low until almost all the liquid has evaporated, then remove from the heat and allow to cool.

3. Place the rice and Shiso Hijiki in a bowl. Use a rice paddle to fold in the Shiso Hijiki.

4. Lightly squeeze out the aburaage juice, then open each half with your fingers (see page 70 for technique). Divide the rice into 8 oblong balls, 2 heaping tablespoons (30 g) each. Stuff a ball into each aburaage half.

5. Place on a serving platter. Serve with Red and White Pickled Ginger, if desired.

TIP: Using apple juice to stew aburaage creates a delightful sweet-and-sour flavor.

PICKLED GINGER AND SESAME SEED INARI

Makes 8 pieces

4 pieces aburaage, prepared the day before

¾ cup plus 1 tablespoon (200 ml) orange juice (see Tip)

2 tablespoons mirin

2 tablespoons Veggie Dashi Soy Sauce (page 98)

1¼ cups (240 g) Basic Sushi Rice (page 6)

¼ cup (50 g) Red and White Pickled Ginger (page 104), julienned

2 teaspoons toasted white sesame seeds

Soy sauce, optional

Dijon mustard, optional

1. Bring water to a boil in a saucepan. Add the aburaage and boil for about 5 minutes to reduce oiliness. Drain, cool, press to remove moisture, and cut in half.

2. Combine the orange juice, mirin, Veggie Dashi Soy Sauce, and aburaage in a saucepan. Simmer until almost all of the liquid has evaporated. Remove from the heat and let cool.

3. Place the rice in a medium bowl and use a rice paddle to fold in the Red and White Pickled Ginger and sesame seeds.

4. Lightly squeeze all moisture from the aburaage, then open each half with your fingers (see page 71 for technique) and flip them inside out. Divide the rice into 8 oblong balls, 2 heaping tablespoons (30 g) each. Stuff one ball into each aburaage.

5. Enjoy as is, or dip in soy sauce mixed with mustard, if desired.

TIP: Stew the aburaage in orange juice for a refreshing citrus flavor.

OPEN INARI

Makes 8 pieces

ABURAAGE

4 pieces aburaage, prepared the day before

¾ cup (180 ml) Veggie Dashi (page 91)

2 tablespoons mirin

2 tablespoons Veggie Dashi Soy Sauce (page 98)

FLAKED SALMON MODOKI

3½ ounces (100 g) fresh okara (soy pulp)

¾ cup (80 g) grated carrot

1 tablespoon sake

¾ teaspoon salt

1 tablespoon flaxseed oil

SCRAMBLED EGG MODOKI

7 ounces (200 g) firm tofu

¼ teaspoon salt

¼ teaspoon turmeric powder

INARI

1¼ cups (240 g) Basic Sushi Rice (page 6)

Pickled Cucumber (page 105), julienned

Shibazuke (page 107), julienned

Takuan (page 105), julienned

1. To prepare the aburaage, bring water to a boil in a saucepan. Add the aburaage and boil for about 5 minutes to reduce oiliness. Drain, cool, press to remove moisture, and cut in half.

2. In a saucepan, combine the Veggie Dashi, mirin, Veggie Dashi Soy Sauce, and aburaage. Simmer on low until almost all the liquid has evaporated. Remove from the heat and let cool.

3. To make the Flaked Salmon Modoki, cook the okara, carrot, sake, and salt in a skillet over low heat. When the mixture develops a flaky consistency, remove from the heat and allow to cool. Stir in the oil.

4. To make the Scrambled Egg Modoki, use your fingers to crumble the tofu into a skillet, then add the salt and turmeric. Heat over medium-high heat until the mixture develops a flaky consistency. Remove from the heat and let cool.

5. To assemble the inarizushi, lightly squeeze out excess moisture from the aburaage and then open each half with your fingers (see page 71 for technique). Divide the rice into 8 oblong balls, 2 tablespoons (30 g) each. Stuff a ball into each aburaage half. Fold down the edge of the aburaage and arrange each modoki on top with Pickled Cucumber, Shibazuke, or Takuan in a colorful way.

TIP: Plain-looking inarizushi can be presented beautifully just by artfully arranging its toppings.

VEGGIE INARI

Makes 10 pieces

4 Japanese mustard spinach (komatsuna)
or mustard green leaves (see Tip)

2 napa cabbage leaves (see Tip)

2 slices red onion, ⅛ inch (2 mm) wide

2 slices watermelon radish or daikon
radish, ⅛ inch (2 mm) wide

2 shiso leaves

1 tablespoon Sushi Vinegar (page 7)

1½ cups (300 g) Basic Sushi Rice (page 6)
with added black rice (see page 5)

Salt

1. Bring water to a boil in a saucepan and sprinkle in some
salt. Blanch the mustard spinach and cabbage for about 5
seconds. Plunge in a bowl of ice water to retain color. Once
cooled, spread them on a paper towel and sprinkle with salt.

2. Place the onion and radish slices on a baking sheet.
Sprinkle with salt, then pour the Sushi Vinegar on top, and
let stand for about 10 minutes.

3. Divide the rice into 10 oblong balls, 2 heaping tablespoons
(30 g) each. Wrap with a mustard spinach, napa cabbage, or
shiso leaf, or top with a slice of onion or radish and secure by
tying mustard spinach stems around the inarizushi.

TIP: Use only the soft, leafy parts of the mustard spinach or
greens and napa cabbage to wrap the sushi.

OSHI

MACKEREL MODOKI OSHI

Makes one 8 x 6 x 2-inch (20 x 15 x 5 cm) "cake"

4½ ounces (120 g) *atsuage* (deep-fried tofu cutlet) or tofu puffs

½ nori sheet

2 teaspoons potato starch

1 tablespoon canola oil

2 tablespoons rice vinegar

1 teaspoon salt, plus more for the daikon

1¼-inch (3 cm) piece dried kombu

9 to 12 thin slices daikon (see Tip)

2 cups (400 g) Basic Sushi Rice (page 6)

Wasabi

Shibazuke (page 107)

1. Place the atsuage in boiling water and boil for about 5 minutes to reduce oiliness. Slice it in half crosswise, then cut according to the area of the bottom of an 8 x 6-inch (20 x 15 cm) pan.

2. Cut the nori slightly longer than the atsuage piece. Dissolve the potato starch in 1 tablespoon water. Brush the mixture on the outside of the atsuage, then cover with the nori.

3. Heat the oil in a skillet over low heat. Grill the nori-covered atsuage with the nori side facing down for about 1 minute. When the nori is crispy, flip and grill for 1 minute.

4. Transfer to a small baking pan. Combine the vinegar and salt and pour over the atsuage and top with the kombu. Fold in plastic wrap and let stand for a couple of hours in the refrigerator.

5. Sprinkle daikon slices with salt to wilt them.

6. Take the atsuage out of the refrigerator and remove the plastic wrap. Spread the rice inside the mold. Add the atsuage on top with the nori side facing up. Cover the top with the daikon. Fold in plastic wrap and refrigerate for 1 hour.

7. Remove the plastic wrap, then slice. Serve with wasabi and Shibazuke.

TIP: Use a mandoline to cut the daikon. Make the slices very thin so they are almost translucent.

ANAKYU MODOKI OSHI:
EEL AND CUCUMBER

Makes one 8 x 6 x 2½-inch (20 x 15 x 6 cm) "cake"

EEL SAUCE

2 tablespoons Veggie Dashi Soy Sauce (page 98)

2 tablespoons mirin

1 tablespoon brown sugar

1 tablespoon sake

OSHI

1 cucumber

Salt

4 slices Eel Modoki (page 22)

¾ cup (150 g) Basic Sushi Rice (page 6)

¾ cup (150 g) Basic Sushi Rice with added black rice (see page 5)

Ground black pepper

1. To make the Eel Sauce, combine all the ingredients in a saucepan. Simmer until it reaches your preferred consistency.

2. To assemble the oshizushi, thinly slice the cucumber lengthwise with a mandoline so that the slices are almost translucent. Sprinkle with salt to wilt.

3. Line the mold with plastic wrap (see Tip). Fill the mold in layers, starting with the Eel Modoki, followed by the regular sushi rice, cucumber, and black rice mix. Firmly press down on the top. Fold in plastic wrap and let stand for a couple of hours in the refrigerator.

4. Cover the mold with a plate, face down, then flip. Pull the plastic wrap to release the mold. Remove the plastic wrap, brush with the sauce, and sprinkle with pepper. Slice and serve.

TIP: Use any mold you like.

BIRTHDAY CAKE MODOKI OSHI

**Makes one 6-inch
(15 cm) round "cake"**

3½ cups (700 g) Basic
Sushi Rice (page 6)

½ batch Scrambled
Egg Modoki (about
3½ ounces/100 g; see
page 77)

1 tablespoon aonori
(dried seaweed flakes)

2 teaspoons shiso
furikake

Daikon

2 shiso leaves

Red and White Pickled
Ginger (page 104)

Tuna Modoki
(page 13)

Squid Modoki
(page 21)

1. Divide the rice into three portions: 1 cup (200 g),
1 cup (200 g), and 1½ cups (300 g). Mix the Scrambled
Egg Modoki into 1 cup of the rice, the aonori into the
remaining 1 cup, and the furikake into the 1½ cups rice.

2. Fill the mold, in three layers, with the rice mixture. Use
a cutting board to press down firmly. Cover with plastic
wrap, then refrigerate for about 1 hour.

3. Use a mandoline to thinly slice the daikon so the slices
are almost translucent, then julienne the slices.

4. Cover the mold with a plate, face down, then flip. Pull
the plastic wrap to release the mold. Arrange the shiso,
daikon, and however much Red and White Pickled Ginger,
Tuna Modoki, and Squid Modoki you'd like on top
(see Tip).

TIP: Top the cake with a rose made of Tuna Modoki and Red
and White Pickled Ginger for a gorgeous presentation.

POKE MODOKI OSHI

Makes one 7-inch (18 cm) angel food "cake"

CURRY & BASIL RICE

1 tablespoon curry powder

¼ cup (60 ml) plus 3 tablespoons Sushi Vinegar (page 7)

1 ounce (30 g) fresh basil leaves (about 1¼ cups)

1½ teaspoons olive oil

1 teaspoon lemon juice

¼ teaspoon salt

1½ cups (300 g) Basic Sushi Rice (page 6), kept warm

POKE MODOKI

1¾ ounces (50 g) dried wakame

Tuna Modoki (page 13)

½ avocado

¼ red onion

1½ teaspoons sesame oil

1½ teaspoons soy sauce

GARNISH

½ teaspoon toasted white sesame seeds

1 scallion

1. To make the Curry & Basil Rice, mix the curry powder and ¼ cup (60 ml) of the Sushi Vinegar in a small bowl.

2. Place the basil, the remaining 3 tablespoons Sushi Vinegar, the olive oil, lemon juice, and salt in a food processor and pulse until smooth.

3. Mix the curry mixture into half of the hot rice. Mix the basil mixture into the remaining half.

4. Line the mold with plastic wrap. Layer the two rice mixtures in the mold, alternating a third of each rice at a time to create your desired pattern. Firmly press down and then fold in the plastic wrap to cover. Let stand for 1 hour in the refrigerator.

5. To make the Poke Modoki, soak the wakame in a bowl of water for 10 minutes, until tender, then drain. Dice the Tuna Modoki, avocado, red onion, and wakame into bite-size pieces. Combine with the remaining ingredients in a bowl.

6. To finish the oshizushi, cut the scallion into 2-inch (5 cm) pieces. Make a slit down the middle of each piece, remove the core, and julienne. Soak in a bowl of ice water.

7. Cover the mold with a plate, face down, then flip. Release the mold. Arrange the Poke Modoki on top (see Tip). Sprinkle with the scallion and sesame seeds and serve.

TIP: Add the Poke Modoki just before serving because moisture might end up seeping through.

SOUPS
AND
STOCKS

VEGGIE DASHI

2-inch (5 cm) piece
dried kombu

1 dried shiitake
mushroom

Combine the kombu and mushroom with 4 cups (1 L) water
in a clean airtight container. Refrigerate overnight. This
keeps for 3 days in the refrigerator.

TIP: Always have some Veggie Dashi on hand—it's used for
many of the recipes in this book!

CLEAR SOUP

Serves 2

2 cups plus 1 tablespoon
(500 ml) Veggie Dashi
(see above)

1 teaspoon soy sauce

½ teaspoon salt

Parsley

Yuzu or lime peel, cut
into ¾-inch (2 cm)
pieces

1. Pour the Veggie Dashi into a saucepan over medium
heat. Once it reaches a gentle boil, add the soy sauce
and salt.

2. Combine as much parsley and yuzu peel as you like in a
soup bowl. Ladle the hot broth into the bowl.

TOMATO MISO SOUP

Serves 2

1⅔ cups (400 ml) Veggie Dashi (page 91)

¾ cup (150 g) diced tomato, fresh or canned

¼ onion, thinly sliced

2 tablespoons hatcho miso or red miso

Finely chopped scallion

1. Combine the Veggie Dashi, tomatoes, and onion in a saucepan over medium heat. Simmer until the onion is cooked through.

2. Add the miso and stir. Ladle into two soup bowls. Top with some scallion.

ROASTED VEGETABLE BROTH

5 ounces (150 g) vegetable scraps (peels, core, stems, etc.; about 1 cup)

1. Preheat the oven to 340°F (170°C). Spread the vegetable scraps out in an oven-safe dish. Bake for 15 to 20 minutes, until tender.

2. Transfer the roasted vegetable scraps to a stockpot with 4 cups (1 L) water. Heat on medium-low for 15 to 20 minutes.

3. Strain out the vegetables and store the broth in a clean jar with a lid. This will keep for 3 days in the refrigerator.

TIP: Roasting concentrates the flavor of the vegetables.

SURF AND TURF MISO SOUP

Serves 2

1⅔ cups (400 ml)
Roasted Vegetable
Broth (page 92)

1½ tablespoons rice
miso

Aosanori or other dried
seaweed (see Tip)

1. Bring the Roasted Vegetable Broth to a boil in a saucepan over medium heat, then add the miso.

2. Add the nori to two soup bowls and then ladle in the soup.

TIP: Once reconstituted, dried seaweed will increase in size by three to five times, so use very small amounts.

MUSHROOM MISO SOUP

Serves 2

1²/₃ cups (400 ml) Veggie Dashi (page 91)

3 ounces (80 g) shiitake mushrooms (about 4)

4 white button mushrooms

2 ounces (50 g) enoki mushrooms (about ¾ cup)

¹/₃ cup (30 g) chopped scallions

3 tablespoons white miso

Thinly sliced red bell pepper

1. Bring the Veggie Dashi to a boil in a saucepan over medium heat. Cut the mushrooms into bite-size pieces and add them to the dashi with the scallions. Simmer until the mushrooms are cooked through.

2. Add the miso. Ladle the mixture into two soup bowls and garnish with the pepper.

ROASTED FISH BONE BROTH MODOKI

Serves 2

1²/₃ cups (400 ml) Roasted Vegetable Broth (page 92)

½ teaspoon sake

½ teaspoon salt

Julienned ginger root

Thinly sliced scallion

1. Bring the Roasted Vegetable Broth to a boil in a saucepan over medium heat, then add the sake and salt.

2. Add the ginger and scallion, then ladle the soup into two bowls.

CONDIMENTS

RED AND WHITE
PICKLED GINGER

TOFU MAYONNAISE

Makes about 2 cups (450 to 500 g)

One 14-ounce (396 g) package silken tofu

½ cup (120 ml) canola oil

2 tablespoons apple cider vinegar

1 teaspoon Dijon mustard

1 teaspoon salt

Remove excess moisture from the tofu using a paper towel. Add all the ingredients to a food processor and pulse until smooth. This will keep for 10 days in an airtight container in the refrigerator.

SPICY MAYONNAISE

Makes about ¼ cup (50 g)

Scant ¼ cup (50 g) Tofu Mayonnaise (see above)

½ teaspoon paprika

¼ teaspoon garlic powder

¼ teaspoon salt

⅛ teaspoon cayenne pepper

⅛ teaspoon ground cumin

Combine all the ingredients and mix well. Transfer to a clean jar with a lid. This will keep for 10 days in the refrigerator.

JAPANESE CHILI OIL

Makes about ½ cup (120 ml)

½-inch (13 mm) piece ginger

Scant ½ cup (100 ml) sesame oil

1 teaspoon ground Sichuan pepper

1 teaspoon red pepper flakes

1. Thinly slice the ginger.

2. Add the ginger and oil to a small saucepan over medium heat.

3. When air bubbles begin to form around the ginger, reduce the heat to low and simmer for about 10 minutes, until the oil has reduced.

4. Combine the Sichuan pepper and red pepper flakes in a clean heat-resistant container. Add the oil and ginger mixture. Let cool. This will keep for 6 months in an airtight container at room temperature.

VEGGIE DASHI SOY SAUCE

Makes 1²/₃ cup (400 ml)

1²/₃ cup (400 ml) soy sauce

2-inch (5 cm) piece dried kombu

2 dried shiitake mushrooms

Combine all the ingredients in a clean jar with a lid. Let stand for a week at room temperature. This will keep for 6 months at room temperature.

KOMBU PONZU

Makes 1¼ cup (280 ml)

¾ cup (180 ml) soy sauce

Scant ½ cup (100 ml) yuzu juice or lemon juice

2-inch (5 cm) piece dried kombu

Combine all the ingredients in a clean jar with a lid. Let stand for a week at room temperature. This will keep for 6 months in the refrigerator.

UMAMI MALTED RICE

Makes 1 cup (120 g)

½ cup plus 2 tablespoons (150 ml) soy sauce

3½ ounces (100 g) fresh malted rice (rice koji)

1. Combine the ingredients in a clean airtight container and shake well.

2. Loosen the lid to allow the mixture to breathe and stir. Let stand at room temperature for about 1 week. This will keep for 6 months in the refrigerator.

CILANTRO SAUCE

Makes 1 cup (150 g)

2½ ounces (70 g) cilantro (about 1 bunch)

1 garlic clove

1¼ cup olive oil

1 tablespoon lemon juice

1 teaspoon salt

Combine all the ingredients along with ¼ cup water in a food processor and pulse until smooth. Transfer to a clean jar with a lid. This will keep for 3 days in the refrigerator.

DAIKON SAUCE

Makes ½ cup (75 g)

2 ounces (60 g) daikon (about ½ cup grated)

1 tablespoon Veggie Dashi Soy Sauce (page 98)

1 tablespoon mirin

1 teaspoon apple cider vinegar

1. Grate the daikon. Combine all the ingredients in a small saucepan over low heat.

2. Once the mixture reaches a gentle boil, remove from the heat. Let cool, then transfer to a jar with a clean lid. This will keep for 3 days in the refrigerator.

TOFU CREAM CHEESE

Makes about 1¼ cups (300 g)

10 ounces (300 g) silken tofu

3½ tablespoons (60 g) rice miso

2 tablespoons (30 g) white miso

1. Remove excess moisture from the tofu with a paper towel and cut into three equal parts. Refrigerate in a colander over a bowl for a few hours to remove moisture.

2. Mix the rice miso and white miso in a small bowl. Remove the tofu from the refrigerator. Coat with the miso mixture and wrap with a clean paper towel. Store in a clean airtight container and refrigerate for 5 days.

3. Remove the paper towel and use or keep refrigerated for up to an additional 10 days.

KOREAN-STYLE SWEET AND SPICY MISO

Makes ½ cup (75 g)

2 tablespoons plus 1 teaspoon rice miso

1 garlic clove, grated

1-inch (2.5 cm) piece ginger, grated

1 tablespoon dark maple syrup

1 tablespoon sesame oil

1 teaspoon gochugaru (Korean chili powder)

Combine all the ingredients along with 2 tablespoons water in a clean jar with a lid. This will keep for 2 weeks in the refrigerator.

SRIRACHA SAUCE

Makes ¾ cup (200 g)

1 medium red bell pepper (about 3½ ounces/100 g), halved lengthwise, stemmed, seeded, and frozen for 8 hours or overnight

2 garlic cloves

Scant ¼ cup (50 g) canned whole peeled tomatoes

2 teaspoons light soy sauce

2 teaspoons apple cider vinegar

1 teaspoon dark maple syrup

1 teaspoon salt

½ teaspoon cayenne pepper

1. Bring a small saucepan of water to a boil. Add the frozen pepper halves, skin side down, to the pan and boil for 10 to 15 minutes, until the skin starts to wrinkle.

2. Transfer to a bowl of ice water to cool. Peel the skin off, beginning at the stem side. Cut lengthwise into four equal parts.

3. Combine all the ingredients in a food processor and pulse until smooth. Transfer to a clean jar with a lid. This will keep for 1 week in the refrigerator.

MAPLE-BALSAMIC SAUCE

KOREAN-STYLE
SWEET AND SPICY MISO

TAPENADE

SRIRACHA SAUCE

MAPLE-BALSAMIC SAUCE

Makes ¼ cup plus 1 tablespoon (50 g)

1½ tablespoons balsamic vinegar

1½ tablespoons dark soy sauce

1 tablespoon dark maple syrup

1 tablespoon olive oil

Combine all the ingredients in a clean jar with a lid and stir. This will keep for 6 months at room temperature.

TAPENADE

Makes scant 1 cup (130 g)

1½ teaspoons (3 g) dried hijiki

2 ounces (60 g) black olives (about a scant half cup canned)

2 tablespoons (15 g) capers

2 tablespoons olive oil

1 tablespoon soy sauce

2 teaspoons lemon juice

Pinch of salt

1. Soak the hijiki in water to reconstitute. Remove excess moisture with a paper towel.

2. Combine all the ingredients in a food processor along with 1 tablespoon water and pulse until smooth. Transfer to a clean jar with a lid. This will keep for 5 days in the refrigerator.

SHISO HIJIKI

Makes ½ cup (100 g)

1 tablespoon (5 g) dried hijiki

2 tablespoons ume plum vinegar or red wine vinegar

1½ teaspoons soy sauce

3 tablespoons plus 1 teaspoon (50 ml) mirin

5 shiso leaves

2 teaspoons toasted white sesame seeds

1. Soak the hijiki in water for 30 minutes to reconstitute. Then drain.

2. Combine the hijiki, vinegar, soy sauce, and mirin in a saucepan. Simmer, stirring occasionally, until the liquid has evaporated, then remove from the heat.

3. Julienne the shiso leaves, then combine with the hijiki and sesame seeds in a bowl.

TIP: Use Shiso Hijiki as a filling for Shiso Hijiki Inari (page 73) or simply as a side for plain rice.

RED AND WHITE PICKLED GINGER

Makes 1⅓ cups (600 g)

RED PICKLED GINGER

10 ounces (300 g) young ginger root

½ cup plus 2 tablespoons (150 ml) ume plum vinegar or red wine vinegar

2 tablespoons apple cider vinegar

2 tablespoons light maple syrup

WHITE PICKLED GINGER

10 ounces (300 g) young ginger root

¾ cup (180 ml) apple cider vinegar

3 tablespoons light maple syrup

3 tablespoons yuzu or lime juice

1 heaping tablespoon salt

1. Use a mandoline to slice the ginger as thinly as possible.

2. Combine the ingredients for each type of pickle in separate, clean, airtight containers. Refrigerate for over a day. These will keep for 1 month in the refrigerator.

TAKUAN: *PICKLED DAIKON*

**Makes 20 ounces
(600 g)**

17 ounces (500 g) daikon

Scant ½ cup (100 ml)
mirin

2 tablespoons brown
sugar

1 tablespoon rice
vinegar

2½ teaspoons salt

½ teaspoon ground
turmeric

1 dried red chile

1 tablespoon uncooked
brown rice

1. Cut the daikon into
wedges ½ inch (1 cm) thick
(see Tip).

2. Combine the mirin, sugar,
vinegar, salt, turmeric, and
chile in a small saucepan
along with a scant ½ cup
(100 ml) water and bring to a
boil. Then remove from the
heat and let cool.

3. Roast the rice in a skillet over medium heat, stirring
constantly. Once the rice starts to pop, remove from
the heat.

4. Combine all the ingredients in a storage bag, remove
the air, and then seal. Refrigerate for a few days. This will
keep for 1 month in the refrigerator.

TIP: Cut the daikon into sticks for use in sushi rolls.

PICKLED CUCUMBER

**Makes 20 ounces
(600 g)**

15 small pickling
cucumbers, such as
gherkins (17 ounces/
500 g)

1 teaspoon salt, plus
more for sprinkling on
the cucumbers

Scant ½ cup (100 ml)
soy sauce

2½ tablespoons (15 g)
julienned ginger

2 heaping tablespoons
brown sugar

1 red chile

1. Cut the cucumbers into slices ¼ inch (5 mm) thick.
Sprinkle with salt and let stand for 20 minutes, then drain
the excess liquid.

2. Combine all of the other ingredients in a small
saucepan over medium heat. Once the sugar dissolves,
add the cucumber slices and increase the heat to high.
When the mixture reaches a gentle boil, remove from the
heat and let cool.

3. Transfer to a storage bag, remove the air, and then
seal. Refrigerate overnight. This will keep for about
1 month in the refrigerator.

PICKLED DAIKON

PICKLED CUCUMBER

SHIBAZUKE (PICKLED
VEGETABLES WITH RED
SHISO LEAVES)

SHIBAZUKE: *PICKLED VEGETABLES WITH RED SHISO LEAVES*

Makes 20 ounces (600 g)

3 Japanese eggplants (10 ounces/300 g)

2 small cucumbers (7 ounces/200 g)

¾ cup (180 ml) ume plum vinegar or red wine vinegar

1 tablespoon plus 1 teaspoon apple cider vinegar

1 ounce (50 g) pickled red shiso leaves

1. Halve the eggplants and cucumbers lengthwise. Slice diagonally into slices ⅛ inch (3 mm) wide.

2. Combine all the ingredients in a storage bag, remove the air, and then seal. Refrigerate for 1 week. This will keep for 1 month in the refrigerator.

QUICK PICKLED
EGGPLANT WITH WASABI

Makes 13 ounces (365 g)

3 Japanese eggplants (10 ounces/300 g)

2-inch piece (3 cm) dried kombu

1 tablespoon mirin

1 teaspoon salt

1 teaspoon wasabi

1. Remove the stem of each eggplant, then slice diagonally into slices ½ inch (15 mm) thick.

2. Combine all the ingredients in a storage bag. Massage from the outside to mix. Remove the air and then seal. Refrigerate overnight. Keep refrigerated and consume within 1 week. The color of the pickled eggplants will darken over time.

TIPS: You can add ¼ teaspoon baking soda to make the eggplant a beautiful purple color.

Use this pickled eggplant as a topping for sushi.

DRINKS

GINGER ORANGE GREEN TEA

Serves 2

2 tablespoons loose green tea leaves

4 slices ginger

Peel of ½ orange (see Tip)

1⅔ cups (400 ml) hot water

Combine all of the ingredients in a teapot or heat-resistant jar and steep for 1 minute.

TIP: A whole mandarin orange peel can be used instead of regular orange peel.

MATCHA LEMONADE

Serves 2

2 teaspoons matcha powder

⅓ cup (50 g) chopped pineapple, in bite-size pieces

1 lemon or lime, sliced

Fresh mint leaves

1⅔ cups (400 ml) seltzer

1. Dissolve the matcha in 1 tablespoon lukewarm water (see Tip), then pour into a glass.

2. Add the pineapple, lemon, and mint to the glass. Add the seltzer. Serve in two glasses.

TIP: Matcha powder is difficult to dissolve, so be sure to use lukewarm water.

AMAZAKE

Serves 4

1 cup (200 g) cooked white short-grain rice

7 ounces (200 g) fresh malted rice (rice koji)

1. Combine the cooked rice with 1²/₃ cups (400 ml) water in a saucepan and cook over low heat to make a rice "porridge."

2. Add the "porridge" and ¾ cup plus 1 tablespoon (200 ml) water to a rice cooker pot. Flake the malted rice and add it to the pot.

3. Turn on the rice cooker and set to warm. Leave the lid open and cover with a damp kitchen towel or paper towel. Warm for 5 to 7 hours. When the mixture tastes sweet, remove from the rice cooker and serve warm. To store, transfer to a clean airtight container. This will keep for 5 days in the refrigerator.

AMAZAKE MATCHA LATTE

Serves 2

¾ cup plus 1 tablespoon (200 ml) Amazake (see above)

1½ teaspoons matcha powder

Combine the ingredients along with ¾ cup plus 1 tablespoon (200 ml) water in a blender and mix until smooth. Pour into two glasses and enjoy.

INDEX

ABOUT THE AUTHOR

iina creates unique and inventive vegan foods that value the natural shapes and colors of vegetables. Her recipes exclude meat, fish, eggs, dairy, and processed white sugar and never use any artificial seasoning or coloring. She is a graduate of L'ecole Vantan culinary school in Tokyo.

In 2008, she lived on Brown's Field, an organic farm in Isumi, Japan. On the farm, while learning to produce and preserve organic foods, she became the chef at Rice Terrace Café. In 2010, she moved to Tokyo and began her career as a vegan chef.

@iina_veganfoodcreator
iina-veganfoodcreator.tumblr.com